MW01489521

THE BIG BOOK OF
CHARLES SPURGEON
QUOTES

Curated by M.K.

"Wisdom is the right use of knowledge. To know is not to be wise. Many men know a great deal, and are all the greater fools for it. There is no fool so great a fool as a knowing fool. But to know how to use knowledge is to have wisdom."

"The Word of God is like a lion. You don't have to defend a lion. All you have to do is let the lion loose, and the lion will defend itself."

"A time will come when instead of shepherds feeding the sheep, the church will have clowns entertaining the goats."

"Whatever a man depends upon, whatever rules his mind, whatever governs his affections, whatever is the chief object of his delight, is his god."

"You may fear that the Lord has passed you by, but it is not so: he who counts the stars, and calls them by their names, is in no danger of forgetting his own children. He knows your case as thoroughly as if you were the only creature he ever made, or the only saint he ever loved. Approach him and be at peace."

"The Bible is not the light of the world, it is the light of the Church. But the world does not read the Bible, the world reads Christians! "You are the light of the world. "."

"You and I cannot be useful if we want to be sweet as honey in the mouths of men. God will never bless us if we wish to please men, that they may think well of us. Are you willing to tell them what will break your own heart in the telling and break theirs in the hearing? If not, you are not fit to serve the Lord. You must be willing to go and speak for God, though you will be rejected."

"You will never know the fullness of Christ until you know the emptiness of everything but Christ."

"My hope lives not because I am not a sinner, but because I am a sinner for whom Christ died; my trust is not that I am holy, but that being unholy, HE is my righteousness. My faith rests not upon what I am or shall be or feel or know, but in what Christ is, in what He has done, and in what He is now doing for me. Hallelujah!"

"If any man thinks ill of you, do not be angry with him, for you are worse than he thinks you to be."

"God is too good to be unkind and He is too wise to be mistaken. And when we cannot trace His hand, we must trust His heart. When you are so weak that you cannot do much more than cry, you coin diamonds with both your eyes. The sweetest prayers God ever hears are the groans and sighs of those who have no hope in anything but his love."

"I believe that one reason why the church of God at this present moment has so little influence over the world is because the world has so much influence over the church."

"My faith rests not in what I am, or shall be, or feel, or know, but in what Christ is, in what he has done, and in what he is doing for me."

"It is not a matter of time so much as a matter of heart; if you have the heart to pray, you will find the time."

"There must be a divorce between you and sin, or there can be no marriage between you and Christ."

"The Word of God is the anvil upon which the opinions of men are smashed."

"Prayer pulls the rope below and the great bell rings above in the ears of God. Some scarcely stir the bell, for they pray so languidly. Others give but an occasional pluck at the rope. But he who wins with heaven is the man who grasps the rope boldly and pulls continuously, with all his might."

"When your will is God's will, you
will have your will."

"We shall not grow weary of waiting upon God if we remember how long and how graciously He once waited for us."

"Whenever God means to make a man great, he always breaks him in pieces first."

"If you wish to know God, you must know his Word. If you wish to perceive His power, you must see how He works by his Word. If you wish to know His purpose before it comes to pass, you can only discover it by His Word."

"When Satan cannot get a great sin in he will let a little one in, like the thief who goes and finds shutters all coated with iron and bolted inside. At last he sees a little window in a chamber. He cannot get in, so he puts a little boy in, that he may go round and open the back door. So the devil has always his little sins to carry about with him to go and open back doors for him, and we let one in and say, 'O, it is only a little one.' Yes, but how that little one becomes the ruin of the entire man!"

"God does not need your strength:
he has more than enough of power
of his own. He asks your weakness:
he has none of that himself, and he
is longing, therefore, to take your
weakness, and use it as the
instrument in his own mighty hand.
Will you not yield your weakness to
him, and receive his strength?"

"A lie can travel half way around the world while the truth is putting on its shoes."

"It's a good thing God chose me before I was born, because he surely would not have afterwards."

"We must all learn to hear what we do not like. The question is not, 'Is it pleasant?' but, 'Is it true?'."

"I have a great need for Christ: I have a great Christ for my need."

"God has so made man's heart that nothing can ever fill it but God himself."

"The greatest enemy to human souls is the self-righteous spirit which makes men look to themselves for salvation."

"It is not how much we have, but how much we enjoy, that makes happiness."

"Beware of no man more than of yourself; we carry our worst enemies within us."

"By perseverance the snail reached the ark."

"If Christ is not all to you He is nothing to you. He will never go into partnership as a part Saviour of men. If He be something He must be everything, and if He be not everything He is nothing to you."

"Faith goes up the stairs that love
has built and looks out the windows
which hope has opened."

"The more you read the Bible; and the more you meditate on it, the more you will be astonished with it."

"May your character not be a writing upon the sand, but an inscription upon the rock!"

"Visit many good books, but live in the Bible."

"A prayerless church member is a hindrance. He is in the body like a rotting bone or a decayed tooth. Before long, since he does not contribute to the benefit of his brethren, he will become a danger and a sorrow to them. Neglect of private prayer is the locust which devours the strength of the church."

"Nearness to God brings likeness to God. The more you see God the more of God will be seen in you."

"I am the subject of depression so fearful that I hope none of you ever get to such extremes of wretchedness as I go to. But I always get back again by this-I know that I trust Christ. I have no reliance but in Him, and if He falls, I shall fall with Him. But if He does not, I shall not. Because He lives, I shall live also, and I spring to my legs again and fight with my depressions of spirit and get the victory through it. And so may you do, and so you must, for there is no other way of escaping from it."

"God works all things together for your good. If the waves roll against you, it only speeds your ship towards the port."

"There is an essential difference between the decease of the godly and the death of the ungodly. Death comes to the ungodly man as a penal infliction, but to the righteous as a summons to his Father's palace. To the sinner it is an execution, to the saint an undressing from his sins and infirmities. Death to the wicked is the King of terrors. Death to the saint is the end of terrors, the commencement of glory."

"Look to the cross, and hate your sin, for sin nailed your Well Beloved to the tree. Look up to the cross, and you will kill sin, for the strength of Jesus' love will make you strong to put down your tendencies to sin."

"God is our portion, Christ our companion, the Spirit our Comforter, Earth our lodge, and Heaven is our home."

"We cannot rely on ourselves, for we have learned by bitter experience the folly of self-confidence. We are compelled to look to the Lord alone. Blessed is the wind that drives the ship into the harbor. Blessed is the distress that forces us to rest in our God."

"The early morning hour should be dedicated to praise: do not the birds set us the example?"

"When you go through a trial, the sovereignty of God is the pillow upon which you lay your head."

"I know of no better thermometer to your spiritual temperature than this, the measure of the intensity of your prayer."

"Hang that question up in your houses, "What would Jesus do?" and then think of another, "How would Jesus do it?" for what he would do, and how he would do it, may always stand as the best guide to us."

"We cannot always trace God's hand but we can always trust God's heart."

"Wherever Jesus may lead us, He goes before us. If we don't know where we are going, we know with whom we go."

"A good character is the best tombstone. Those who loved you and were helped by you will remember you when forget-me-nots have withered. Carve your name on hearts, not on marble."

"Every generation needs regeneration."

"A village is a hive of glass, where nothing unobserved can pass."

"Anything is a blessing which makes us pray."

"Oh, my brothers and sisters in Christ, if sinners will be damned, at least let them leap to hell over our bodies; and if they will perish, let them perish with our arms about their knees, imploring them to stay, and not madly to destroy themselves. If hell must be filled, at least let it be filled in the teeth of our exertions, and let not one go there unwarned and unprayed for."

"It was God's word that made us; is it any wonder that His word should sustain us?"

"Let your cares drive you to God. I shall not mind if you have many of them if each one leads you to prayer. If every fret makes you lean more on the Beloved, it will be a benefit."

"If you can sin and not weep over it, you are an heir of Hell. If you can go into sin, and afterwards feel satisfied to have done so, you are on the road to destruction. If there are no prickings of conscience, no inward torments, no bleeding wounds; if you have no throbs and heavings of a bosom that cannot rest; if your soul never feels filled with wormwood and gall when you know you have done evil, you are no child of God."

"Defend the Bible? I'd sooner defend a lion. You don't defend the Bible; you open its cage and let it roar."

"I believe that the happiest of all Christians and the truest of Christians are those who never dare to doubt God, but take His Word simply as it stands, and believe it, and ask no questions, just feeling assured that if God has said it, it will be so."

"When a man is saved by divine grace, he is not wholly cleansed from the corruption of his heart. When we believe in Jesus Christ all our sins are pardoned; yet the power of sin, albeit that it is weakened and kept under by the dominion of the new-born nature which God doth infuse into our souls, doth not cease, but still tarrieth in us, and will do so to our dying day."

"It is a good rule never to look into the face of a man in the morning till you have looked into the face of God."

"God helps those who cannot help themselves."

"Have your heart right with Christ, and he will visit you often, and so turn weekdays into Sundays, meals into sacraments, homes into temples, and earth into heaven."

"Every growth of spiritual life, from the first tender shoot until now, has been the work of the Holy Spirit. The only way to more life is the Holy Spirit. You will not even know that you want more unless He works in you to desire it. The Spirit of God must come and make the letter alive, transfer it to your heart, set it on fire, and make it burn within you, or else its divine force and majesty will be hid from your eyes. Prayer is the creation of the Holy Spirit. We cannot do without prayer, and we cannot pray without the Holy Spirit."

"Patience! patience! You are always in a hurry, but God is not."

"Right is right though all condemn, and wrong is wrong though all approve."

"Those who think that a woman detained at home by her little family is doing nothing, think the reverse of what is true. Scarcely can the godly mother quit her home for a place of worship; but dream not that she is lost to the work of the church; far from it, she is doing the best possible service for her Lord. Mothers, the godly training of your offspring is your first and most pressing duty."

"A person who is really saved by Grace does not need to be told that he is under solemn obligations to serve Christ. The new life within him tells him that. Instead of regarding it as a burden, he gladly surrenders himself, body, soul, and spirit, to the Lord."

"A child of God should be a visible beatitude for joy and happiness, and a living doxology for gratitude and adoration."

"If you have to give a carnival to get people to come to church, then you will have to keep giving carnivals to keep them coming back."

"Morality may keep you out of jail,
but it takes the blood of Jesus Christ
to keep you out of hell."

"The Bible in the memory is better than the Bible in the book case."

"When we believe that we ought to be satisfied, rather than God glorified, we set God below ourselves, imagine that He should submit His own honor to our advantage; we make ourselves more glorious than God, as though we were not made for Him, but He made for us; this is to have a very low esteem of the majesty of God."

"You will never glory in God till first of all God has killed your glorying in yourself."

"Christians are not so much in danger when they are persecuted as when they are admired."

"God gave us sleep to remind us we are not him."

"Atheism is a strange thing. Even the devils never fell into that vice."

"O child of God, be more careful to keep the way of the Lord, more concentrated in heart in seeking His glory, and you will see the loving-kindness and the tender mercy of the Lord in your life."

"My friends, it is one thing to go to church or chapel; it is quite another thing to go to God."

"Unless you have forgiven others you read your own death warrant when you repeat the Lord's Prayer."

"If Christ has died for me, ungodly as I am, without strength as I am, then I cannot live in sin any longer. I must arouse myself to love and serve Him who has redeemed me. I cannot trifle with the evil that killed my best Friend. I must be holy for His sake. How can I live in sin when He has died to save me from it?"

"Trials teach us what we are; they dig up the soil, and let us see what we are made of."

"Nobody ever outgrows Scripture; the book widens and deepens with our years."

"It is no novelty, then, that I am preaching; no new doctrine. I love to proclaim these strong old doctrines, that are called by nickname Calvinism, but which are surely and verily the revealed truth of God as it is in Christ Jesus."

"Groanings which cannot be uttered are often prayers which cannot be refused."

"Mind how you pray. Make real business of it. Let it never be a dead formality. plead the promise in a truthful, business-like way. Ask for what you want, because the Lord has promised it. Believe that you have the blessing, and go forth to your work in full assurance of it. Go from your knees singing, because the promise is fulfilled: thus will your prayer be answered. the strength [not length] of your prayer. wins. God; and the strength of prayer lies in your faith in the promise which you pleaded before the Lord."

"I believe that nothing happens apart from divine determination and decree. We shall never be able to escape from the doctrine of divine predestination - the doctrine that God has foreordained certain people unto eternal life."

"That very church which the world likes best is sure to be that which God abhors."

"Growing a beard is a habit most natural, Scriptural, manly and beneficial."

"If heaven were by merit, it would never be heaven to me, for if I were in it I should say, "I am sure I am here by mistake; I am sure this is not my place; I have no claim to it. " But if it be of grace and not of works, then we may walk into heaven with boldness."

"A man says to me, 'Can you explain the seven trumpets of the Revelation?' No, but I can blow one in your ear, and warn you to escape from the wrath to come."

"Think not of the sinner or the greatness of his sin, but think of the greatness of the Savior!"

"Avoid a sugared gospel as you would shun sugar of lead. Seek the gospel which rips up and tears and cuts and wounds and hacks and even kills, for that is the gospel that makes alive again. And when you have found it, give good heed to it. Let it enter into your inmost being. As the rain soaks into the ground, so pray the Lord to let his gospel soak into your soul."

"Before you go out into the world, wash your face in the clear crystal of praise. Bury each yesterday in the fine linen and spices of thankfulness."

"If you cannot trust God for the temporal, how dare you trust him for the eternal?"

"Every Christian is either a missionary or an imposter."

"Answering a student's question, 'Will the heathen who have not heard the Gospel be saved?' thus, 'It is more a question with me whether we, who have the Gospel and fail to give it to those who have not, can be saved."

"A well marked Bible is the sign of a well-fed soul."

"If you want the truth to go round the world you must hire an express train to pull it; but if you want a lie to go round the world it will fly; it is as light as a feather, and a breath will carry it."

"Time is short. Eternity is long. It is only reasonable that this short life be lived in the light of eternity."

"Child of God, you cost Christ too much for him to forget you."

"Every Christian man has a choice between being humble and being humbled."

"Preach Christ or nothing: don't dispute or discuss except with your eye on the cross."

"Our great object of glorifying God is to be mainly achieved by the winning of souls Do not close a single sermon without addressing the ungodly."

"Jesus wept, but He never complained."

"The Lord gets his best soldiers out of the highlands of affliction."

"Economy is half the battle in life, but it is not so hard to earn money as to spend it well. Hundreds would never have known want if they had not first known waste."

"If you simply take the name of Christ upon you and call yourself His servant, yet do not obey Him, but follow your own whim, or your own hereditary prejudice, or the custom of some erroneous church- you are no servant of Christ. If you really are a servant of Christ, your first duty is to obey Him."

"It does not spoil your happiness to confess your sin. The unhappiness is in not making the confession."

"We should pray when we are in a praying mood, for it would be sinful to neglect so fair an opportunity. We should pray when we are not in a proper mood, for it would be dangerous to remain in so unhealthy a condition."

"I have now concentrated all my prayers into one, and that one prayer is this, that I may die to self, and live wholly to Him."

"Let no Christian parents fall into the delusion that Sunday School is intended to ease them of their personal duties. The first and most natural condition of things is for Christian parents to train up their own children in the nurture and admonition of the Lord."

"Some go to church to take a walk; some go there to laugh and talk. Some go there to meet a friend; some go there their time to spend. Some go there to meet a lover; some go there a fault to cover. Some go there for speculation; some go there for observation. Some go there to doze and nod; the wise go there to worship God."

"If Christ has died for me, I cannot trifle with the evil that killed my best Friend."

"When joy and prayer are married,
their first born child is gratitude."

"When I am weak then am I strong, Grace is my shield and Christ my Song."

"I believe the hard heartest, most cross grained and most unloving Christians in all the world are those who have not had much trouble in their life. And those that are the most sympathizing, loving and Christlike are generally those who have the most affliction. The worse thing that can happen to any of us is to have a path made too smooth. One of the greatest blessings the Lord ever gave us was a cross."

"The best way to live above all fear of death is to die every morning before you leave your bedroom."

"God's thoughts of you are many, let not yours be few in return."

"Have you no wish for others to be saved? Then you're not saved yourself, be sure of that!"

"The only real argument against the Bible is an unholy life. When a man argues against the Word of God, follow him home, and see if you cannot discover the reason of his enmity to the Word of the Lord. It lies in some sort of sin."

"I saw a young sister, just before this service; and I said to her, "When did you find the Lord?" She replied, "It was when I was very ill. " Yes, it is often so; God makes us ill in body that we may have time to think of Him, and turn to Him. What would become of some people if they were always in good health, or if they were always prospering? But tribulation is the black dog that goes after the stray sheep, and barks them back to the Good Shepherd. I thank God that there are such things as the visitations of correction and of holy discipline, to preserve our spirit, and bring us to Christ."

"Begin early to teach, for children begin early to sin."

"To trust God in the light is nothing, but trust him in the dark- that is faith."

"This is the doctrine that we preach; if a man be saved, all the honor is to be given to Christ; but if a man be lost, all the blame is to be laid upon himself. You will find all true theology summed up in these two short sentences, salvation is all of the grace of God, damnation is all of the will of man."

"There is no form of sinfulness to which you are addicted which Christ cannot remove."

"My entire theology can be condensed into four words, 'JESUS DIED FOR ME'."

"The repetition of small efforts will accomplish more than the occasional use of great talents."

"Satan always hates Christian fellowship; it is his policy to keep Christians apart. Anything which can divide saints from one another he delights in. He attaches far more importance to godly intercourse than we do. Since union is strength, he does his best to promote separation."

"When God places a burden upon you, He places His arms underneath you."

"God's mercy is so great that you may sooner drain the sea of its water, or deprive the sun of its light, or make space too narrow, than diminish the great mercy of God."

"Trust Christ, but do not trust yourself."

"A Bible that's falling apart usually belongs to someone who isn't."

"If I am not today all that I hope to be, yet I see Jesus, and that assures me that I shall one day be like Him."

"There is no university for a Christian, like that of sorrow and trial."

"The seasons change and you change, but the Lord abides evermore the same, and the streams of His love are as deep, as broad and as full as ever."

"I heard the story of a man, a blasphemer. an atheist, who was converted singularly by a sinful action of his. He had written on a piece of paper, "God is nowhere," and ordered his child to read it, for he would make him an atheist too. The child spelled it, "God is n-o-w h-e-r-e. God is now here. " It was a truth instead of a lie, and the arrow pierced the man's own heart."

"We are not to be alarmed when Satan hinders us, for it is proof that we are on the Lord's side and are doing the Lord's work. In His strength, we will win the victory and triumph over our adversary."

"You cannot preach conviction of sin unless you have suffered it. You cannot preach repentance unless you have practiced it. You cannot preach faith unless you have exercised it. True preaching is artesian; it wells up from the great depths of the soul. If Christ has not made a well within us, there will be no outflow from us."

"If the devil never roars, the Church will never sing! God is not doing much if the devil is not awake and busy. Depend upon it: a working Christ makes a raging devil! When you hear ill reports, cruel speeches, threats, taunts and the like, believe that the Lord is among His people and is working gloriously."

"A little faith will bring your soul to heaven; a great faith will bring heaven to your soul."

"Care more for a grain of faith than
a ton of excitement."

"The Christian should work as if all depended upon him, and pray as if it all depended upon God."

"I have learned to kiss the waves that throw me up against the Rock of Ages."

"Never try to live on the old manna, nor seek to find help in Egypt. All must come from Jesus or thou art undone forever. Old anointings will not suffice to impart unction to thy spirit; thine head must have fresh oil poured upon it from the golden horn of the sanctuary, or it will cease from its glory."

"If a man can preach one sermon without mentioning Christ's name in it, it ought to be his last."

"The mind of God is greater than all the minds of men, so let all men leave the gospel just as God has delivered it unto us."

"You say, 'If I had a little more, I should be very satisfied. ' You make a mistake. If you are not content with what you have, you would not be satisfied if it were doubled."

"He that knows how to overcome the Lord in prayer, has heaven and earth at his disposal."

"Soul-winning is the chief business of the Christian minister; it should be the main pursuit of every true believer."

"Without the Spirit of God, we can do nothing. We are as ships without wind. We are useless."

"I am persuaded that men think there is no God because they wish there were none. They find it hard to believe in God, and to go on in sin, so they try to get an easy conscience by denying his existence."

"Prayer can never be in excess."

"Sincerity makes the very least person to be of more value than the most talented hypocrite."

"There is hardship in everything except eating pancakes."

"A rejoicing heart soon makes a praising tongue."

"The Christian life is very much like climbing a hill of ice. You cannot slide up, nay, you have to cut every step with an ice axe; only with incessant labor in cutting and chipping can you make any progress. If you want to know how to backslide, leave off going forward. Cease going upward and you will go downward of necessity. You can never stand still."

"The day we find the perfect church,
it becomes imperfect the moment
we join it."

"Prayer and praise are the oars by which a man may row his boat into the deep waters of the knowledge of Christ."

"Is it not an amazing fact that while others leave us and forsake us, that God never does?"

"Do you find it difficult to forgive one who has wronged you? Then you will find it difficult to get to heaven."

"O man, I beseech you do not treat God's promises as if they were curiosities for a museum; but use them as every day sources of comfort. Trust the Lord whenever your time of need comes on."

"The law is for the self-righteous, to humble their pride: the gospel is for the lost, to remove their despair."

"Be thankful for the thorns and thistles, which keep you from being in love with this world, and becoming an idolater."

"We shall never see much change for the better in our churches in general till the prayer meeting occupies a higher place in the esteem of Christians."

"Every man needs a blind eye and a deaf ear, so when people applaud, you'll only hear half of it, and when people salute, you'll only see part of it. Believe only half the praise and half the criticism."

"The word of God is always most precious to the man who most lives upon it."

"I believe that much of the secret of soul-winning lies in having bowels of compassion, in having spirits that can be touched with the feeling of human infirmities."

"You may readily judge whether you are a child of God or a hypocrite by seeing in what direction your soul turns in seasons of severe trial. The hypocrite flies to the world and finds a sort of comfort there. But the child of God runs to his Father and expects consolation only from the Lord's hand."

"Every hour of every day, God is richly blessing us; both when we sleep and when we wake His mercy waits upon us."

"Winners of souls must first be weepers for souls."

"Great hearts can only be made by great troubles. Great faith must have great trials."

"Lord, send Your life throughout the entire church. Visit Your church; restore sound doctrine and holy, earnest living. Take away from professing Christians their love of frivolities, their attempts to meet the world on it's own ground, and give back the old love of the doctrines of the Cross and Christ. May free grace and dying love again be the music that refreshes the church and makes her heart exceeding glad."

"Discernment is not a matter of telling the difference between right and wrong; rather it is telling the difference between right and almost right."

"True prayer is measured by weight, not by length. A single groan before God may have more fullness of prayer in it than a fine oration of great length."

"Within the Scripture there is a balm for every wound, a salve for every sore."

"Soar back through all your own experiences. Think of how the Lord has led you in the wilderness and has fed and clothed you every day. How God has borne with your ill manners, and put up with all your murmurings and all your longings after the 'sensual pleasures of Egypt!' Think of how the Lord's grace has been sufficient for you in all your troubles."

"If we want revivals, we must revive our reverence for the Word of God."

"Sin is a thing of time, but mercy is from everlasting. Transgression is but of yesterday, but mercy was ever of old. Before you and I sought the Lord, the Lord sought us."

"Nothing can damn a man but his own righteousness; nothing can save him but the righteousness of Christ."

"If you profess to be a Christian, yet find full satisfaction in worldly pleasures and pursuits, your profession is false."

"One of the greatest rewards that we ever receive for serving God is the permission to do still more for Him."

"Scripture is like a lion. Who ever heard of defending a lion? Just turn it loose; it will defend itself."

"Many people are born crying, live complaining, and die disappointed; they chew the bitter pill which they would not even know to be bitter if they had the sense to swallow it whole in a cup of patience and water."

"In prosperity God is heard, and that is a blessing; but in adversity God is seen, and that is a greater blessing."

"The Word of God is a lamp by night, a light by day, and a delight at all times."

"You are as much serving God in looking after your own children, & training them up in God's fear, & minding the house, & making your household a church for God, as you would be if you had been called to lead an army to battle for the Lord of hosts."

"Brethren, do something; do something, do something! While societies and unions make constitutions, let us win souls. I pray you, be men of action all of you. Get to work and quit yourselves like men. Old Suvarov's idea of war is mine: `Forward and strike! No theory! Attack! Form a column! Charge bayonets! Plunge into the center of the enemy! Our one aim is to win souls; and this we are not to talk about, but do in the power of God!'."

"To be a soul winner is the happiest thing in the world. And with every soul you bring to Jesus Christ, you seem to get a new heaven here upon earth."

"None are more unjust in their judgments of others than those who have a high opinion of themselves."

"As sure as God puts His children in the furnace of affliction, He will be with them in it."

"To be a soul winner is the happiest thing in this world."

"The true way for a Christian to live is to live entirely upon Christ. Christians have experiences and they have feelings, but, if they are wise, they never feed upon these things, but upon Christ, Himself."

"Ten minutes praying is better than
a year's murmuring."

"It is a remarkable fact that all the heresies which have arisen in the Christian Church have had a decided tendency to dishonor God and to flatter man."

"Remember that thought is speech
before God."

"But the best argument of all [for evangelism] is to be found in the wounds of Jesus. You want to honor Him, you desire to put many crowns upon His head, and this you can best do by winning souls for Him. These are the spoils that He covets, these are the trophies for which He fights, these are the jewels that shall be His best adornment."

"A sinner can no more repent and believe without the Holy Spirit's aid than he can create a world."

"A Jesus who never wept could never wipe away my tears."

"Not that our salvation should be the effect of our work, but our work should be the evidence of our salvation."

"A man is not saved against his will, but he is made willing by the operation of the Holy Ghost. A mighty grace which he does not wish to resist enters into the man, disarms him, makes a new creature of him, and he is saved."

"It is the whole business of the whole church to preach the whole gospel to the whole world."

"His eyes never slumber, and His hands never rest; His heart never ceases to beat with love, and His shoulders are never weary of carrying His people's burdens."

"Faith and works are bound up in the same bundle. He that obeys God trusts God; and he that trusts God obeys God. He that is without faith is without works; and he that is without works is without faith."

"The glory of God's faithfulness is
that no sin of ours has ever made
Him unfaithful."

"The devil is not afraid of a dust-covered Bible."

"I do not think the devil cares how many churches you build, if only you have lukewarm preachers and people in them."

"He who does not serve God where he is would not serve God anywhere else."

"My soul has learned yet more fully than ever, this day, that there is no satisfaction to be found in earthly things-God alone can give rest to my spirit."

"Nobody can do as much damage to the church of God as the man who is within its walls, but not within its life."

"Satan can make men dance upon the brink of hell as though they were on the verge of heaven."

"The more holy a man becomes, the more conscious he is of unholiness."

"Consume all obstacles, heavenly fire, and give us now both hearts of flame and tongues of fire to preach Your reconciling word, for Jesus' sake."

"Thus there will be three effects of nearness to Jesus humility, happiness, and holiness."

"No man can do me a truer kindness
in this world than to pray for me."

"Our Lord Jesus is ever giving, and does not for a solitary instant withdraw his hand. As long as there is a vessel of grace not yet full to the brim, the oil shall not be stayed. He is a sun ever-shining; he is manna always falling round the camp; he is a rock in the desert, ever sending out streams of life from his smitten side; the rain of his grace is always dropping; the river of his bounty is ever-flowing, and the well-spring of his love is constantly overflowing."

"Prayer meetings are the throbbing machinery of the church."

"When preaching and private talk are not available, you need to have a tract ready. Get good striking tracts, or none at all. But a touching gospel tract may be the seed of eternal life. Therefore, do not go out without your tracts."

"Give me great sinners to make great saints! They are glorious raw material for Grace to work upon and when you do get them saved, they will shake the very gates of Hell!"

"The bridge of grace will bear your weight, brother. Thousands of big sinners have gone across that bridge, yea, tens of thousands have gone over it. Some have been the chief of sinners and some have come at the very last of their days but the arch has never yielded beneath their weight. I will go with them trusting to the same support. It will bear me over as it has for them."

"God alone can do what seems impossible. This is the promise of his grace: 'I will restore to you the years that the swarming locust has eaten' (Joel 2:25). God can give back all those years of sorrow, and you will be the better for them. God will grind sunlight out of your black nights. In the oven of affliction, grace will prepare the bread of delight. Someday you will thank God for all your sadness."

"A godly man often grows best when his worldly circumstances decay. He who follows Christ for his bag is a Judas; they who follow for loaves and fishes are children of the devil; but they who attend Him out of love to Himself are His own beloved ones. Lord, let me find my life in Thee, and not in the mire of this world's favour or gain."

"It is blessed to eat into the very soul of the Bible until, at last, you come to talk in Scriptural language, and your very style is fashioned upon Scripture models, and, what is better still, your spirit is flavored with the words of the Lord. Prick him anywhere; and you will find that his blood is Bibline, the very essence of the Bible flows from him."

"If you have no wish to bring others to heaven, you are not going there yourself."

"The child of God knows his good works do not make him acceptable to God, for he was acceptable to God by Jesus Christ long before he had any good works."

"Let gratitude be awakened; let humility be deepened; let love be quickened."

"To pray is to mount on eagle's wings above the clouds and get into the clear heaven where God dwelleth."

"No man ever served God by doing things tomorrow."

"I do believe we slander Christ when we think we are to draw the people by something else but the preaching of Christ crucified."

"I would not give much for your religion unless it can be seen. Lamps do not talk, but they do shine."

"Lord, let me find my life in thee, and not in the mire of this world's favour or gain."

"The more objects you set your heart upon, the more thorns there are to tear your peace of mind to shreds."

"If you will not have death unto sin, you shall have sin unto death. There is no alternative. If you do not die to sin, you shall die for sin. If you do not slay sin, sin will slay you."

"Neglect of private prayer is the locust which devours the strength of the church."

"God save us from living in comfort
while sinners are sinking into hell!"

"Train your child in the way in which you know you should have gone yourself."

"Free will carried many a soul to hell, but never a soul to heaven."

"Stale godliness is ungodliness. Let our religion be as warm, and constant, and natural as the flow of the blood in our veins. A living God must be served in a living way."

"Some Christians try to go to heaven alone, in solitude; but believers are not compared to bears, or lions, or other animals that wander alone; but those who belong to Christ are sheep in this respect, that they love to get together. Sheep go in flocks, and so do God's people."

"Sin and Hell are married unless repentance proclaims the divorce."

"You cannot be Christ's servant if you are not willing to follow him, cross and all. What do you crave? A crown? Then it must be a crown of thorns if you are to be like him. Do you want to be lifted up? So you shall, but it will be upon a cross."

"Prayer moves the arm that moves the world."

"We declare, upon Scriptural authority, that the human will is so desperately set on mischief, so depraved, and so inclined to everything that is evil, and so disinclined to everything that is good, that without the powerful, supernatural, irresistible influence of the Holy Spirit, no human will ever be constrained towards Christ."

"The sermon which does not lead to Christ, or of which Jesus Christ is not the top and the bottom, is a sort of sermon that will make the devils in hell laugh, but make the angels of God weep."

"Mighty prayer has often been
produced by mighty trial."

"God has not made this world to be a nest for us, and if we try to make it such for ourselves, he plants thorns in it, so that we may be compelled to mount and find our soul's true home somewhere else, in a higher and nobler sphere than this poor world can give."

"You and your sins must separate,
or you and your God will never
come together."

"To wash and dress a corpse is a far different thing from making it alive: Man can do the one-God alone can do the other."

"It is far easier to fight with sin in public than to pray against it in private."

"Preach not calmly and quietly as though you were asleep, but preach with fire and pathos and passion."

"A man who does nothing never has time to do anything."

"Doth not all nature around me praise God? If I were silent, I should be an exception to the universe. Doth not the thunder praise Him as it rolls like drums in the march of the God of armies? Do not the mountains praise Him when the woods upon their summits wave in adoration? Doth not the lightning write His name in letters of fire? Hath not the whole earth a voice? And shall I, can I, silent be?"

"He that is never on his knees on earth shall never stand upon his feet in heaven."

"It is the burning lava of the soul that has a furnace within-a very volcano of grief and sorrow-it is that burning lava of prayer that finds its way to God. No prayer ever reaches God's heart which does not come from our hearts."

"If any of you should ask me for an epitome of the Christian religion, I should say that it is in one word - prayer. Live and die without prayer, and you will pray long enough when you get to hell."

"As soon as a man has found Christ,
he begins to find others."

"He (Jesus) will reign over you, either by your consent, or without it."

"Six feet of dirt make all men equal."

"I would rather teach one man to pray than ten men to preach."

"Depend on it, my hearer, you never will go to heaven unless you are prepared to worship Jesus Christ as God."

"Some temptations come to the industrious, but all temptations attack the idle."

"To pursue union at the expense of truth is treason to the Lord Jesus."

"There is no other place where the heart should be so free as before the mercy seat. There, you can talk out your very soul, for that is the best prayer that you can present. Do not ask for what some tell you that you should ask for, but for that which you feel the need of, that which the Holy Spirit has made you to hunger and to thirst for, you ask for that."

"When you have no helpers, see your helpers in God. When you have many helpers, see God in all your helpers. When you have nothing but God, see all in God. When you have everything, see God in everything. Under all conditions, stay thy heart only on the Lord."

"Calvinism did not spring from Calvin. We believe that it sprang from the great Founder of all truth."

"It is wonderful how God works by our hands, and yet His own hand does it all."

"Do not go on His errands till first you have sat at His feet."

"When you think of what you are, and despair; think also of what He is, and take heart."

"Remember the goodness of God in the frost of adversity."

"My brethren, do you believe in the Holy Ghost?. Have we such a reliance upon the Holy Ghost? Do we believe that, at this moment, He can clothe us with power, even as He did the apostles at Pentecost? Do we believe that, under our preaching, by His energy a thousand might be born in a day?"

"When you are instructed by affliction, you can become a comforter to the afflicted."

"If God lights the candle, none can blow it out."

"When I thought God was hard, I found it easy to sin; but when I found God so kind, so good, so overflowing with compassion, I smote upon my breast to think that I could ever have rebelled against One who loved me so, and sought my good."

"He that reads his Bible to find fault with it will soon discover that the Bible finds fault with him."

"If I had a brother who had been murdered, what would you think of me if I. daily consorted with the assassin who drove the dagger into my brother's heart; surely I too must be an accomplice in the crime. Sin murdered Christ; will you be a friend to it? Sin pierced the heart of the Incarnate God; can you love it?"

"See yonder another King's garden, which the King waters with his bloody sweat-Gethsemane, whose bitter herbs are sweeter far to renewed souls than even Eden's luscious fruits. There the mischief of the serpent in the first garden was undone: there the curse was lifted from earth, and borne by the woman's promised seed."

"I believe that many professing Christians are cold and uncomfortable because they are doing nothing for their Lord; but if they actively served him, their blood would begin to circulate spiritually, and it would be well with them."

"We are one in Christ; let us be friends with one another; but let us never be friends with one another's error. If I be wrong, rebuke me sternly; I can bear it, and bear it cheerfully; and if ye be wrong, expect the like measure from me, and neither peace nor parley with your mistakes."

"The grace that does not change my life will not save my soul."

"This day, my God, I hate sin not because it damns me, but because it has done Thee wrong. To have grieved my God is the worst grief to me."

"God is to be praised with the voice,
and the heart should go therewith
in holy exultation."

"When we preach Christ crucified, we have no reason to stammer, or stutter, or hesitate, or apologize; there is nothing in the gospel of which we have any cause to be ashamed."

"If you take Christ out of Christianity, Christianity is dead. If you remove grace out of the gospel, the gospel is gone. If the people do not like the doctrine of grace, give them all the more of it."

"Hope itself is like a star- not to be seen in the sunshine of prosperity, and only to be discovered in the night of adversity."

"It is the habit of faith, when she is praying, to use pleas. Mere prayer sayers, who do not pray at all, forget to argue with God; but those who prevail bring forth their reasons and their strong arguments."

"The Word of God will be to you a bulwark and a high tower, a castle of defense against the foe. Oh, see to it that the Word of God is in you, in your very soul, permeating your thoughts, and so operating upon your outward life, that all may know you to be a true Bible-Christian, for they perceive it in your words and deeds."

"Shall I give you yet another reason why you should pray? I have preached my very heart out. I could not say any more than I have said. Will not your prayers accomplish that which my preaching fails to do? Is it not likely that the Church has been putting forth its preaching hand but not its praying hand? Oh dear friends! Let us agonize in prayer."

"Of two evils, choose neither."

"When the time comes for you to die, you need not be afraid, because death cannot separate you from God's love."

"Those who dive in the sea of affliction bring up rare pearls."

"The power of prayer can never be overrated. They who cannot serve God by preaching need not regret. If a man can but pray he can do anything. He who knows how to overcome with God in prayer has Heaven and earth at his disposal."

"Trials make more room for consolation. There is nothing that makes a man have a big heart like a great trial. I always find that little, miserable people, whose hearts are about the size of a grain of mustard seed, never have had much to try them. I have found that those people who have no sympathy for their fellows — who never weep for the sorrows of others — very seldom have had any woes of their own. Great hearts can only be made by great troubles."

"There is no attribute of God more comforting to His children than the doctrine of Divine Sovereignty. Under the most adverse circumstances, in the most severe troubles, they believe that Sovereignty hath ordained their afflictions, that Sovereignty overrules them, and that Sovereignty will sanctify them all."

"The disciples of a patient Saviour
should be patient themselves."

"Only the prayer which comes from our heart can get to God's heart."

"If you are to go to Christ, do not put on your good doings and feelings, or you will get nothing. Go in your sins, they are your livery. Your ruin is your argument for mercy! Your poverty is your plea for heavenly alms! And your need is the motive for heavenly goodness."

"Anger does a man more hurt than
that which made him angry."

"If there be any one point in which the Christian church ought to keep its fervor at a white heat, it is concerning missions. If there be anything about which we cannot tolerate lukewarmness,it is the matter of sending the gospel to a dying world."

"Without Christ there is no hope."

"Ah, Lord Jesus! I never knew Your love till I understood the meaning of Your death."

"Man was made in the image of God, and nothing will satisfy man but God, in whose image he was made."

"It seems odd, that certain men who talk so much of what the Holy Spirit reveals to themselves, should think so little of what he has revealed to others."

"If we complained less, and praised more, we should be happier, and God would be more glorified."

"Grace does not choose a man and leave him as he is."

"I would sooner be holy than happy if the two things could be divorced. Were it possible for a man always to sorrow and yet to be pure, I would choose the sorrow if I might win the purity, for to be free from the power of sin, to be made to love holiness, is true happiness."

"Those who do not hope cannot wait; but if we hope for that we see not, then do we with patience wait for it."

"Faith is the accepting of what God gives. Faith is the believing what God says. Faith is the trusting to what Jesus has done. Only do this and you are saved, as surely as you are alive!"

"It is a terribly easy matter to be a minister of the gospel and a vile hypocrite at the same time."

"Praying without fervency is like hunting with a dead dog."

"When all else is changing within and around, in God and His mercy no change can be found."

"The goal of prayer is the ear of God."

"The greater our present trials, the louder will our future songs be, and the more intense our joyful gratitude."

"Repentance and faith are distasteful to the unregenerate; they would sooner repeat a thousand formal prayers than shed a solitary tear of true repentance."

"Sincere repentance is continual.
Believers repent until their dying
day. This dropping well is not
intermittent."

"It is folly to think the Lord provides grace for every trouble but the one you are in today."

"When we come to the end of self we come to the beginning of Christ."

"True prayer is measured by weight,
not by length."

"As the rain soaks into the ground,
so pray the Lord to let his gospel
soak into your soul."

"Faith is a principle which hath its root deeper feeling. We believe, whether we see or not."

"Beware of self-righteousness. The black devil of licentiousness destroys his hundreds, but the white devil of self-righteousness destroys his thousands."

"Be deaf, be blind, be dead to gossip, and it will grow disgusted with you and select a more sensitive victim."

"Pray for the peace of Jerusalem and thine own soul shall be refreshed."

"The best style of prayer is that which cannot be called anything else but a cry."

"The condition of the church may be very accurately gauged by its prayer meetings. So is the prayer meeting a grace-ometer, and from it we may judge of the amount of divine working among a people. If God be near a church, it must pray. And if He be not there, one of the first tokens of His absence will be slothfulness in prayer."

"It is said that our anxiety does not empty tomorrow of its sorrows, but only empties today of its strength."

"Praise is the Rehearsal of Our eternal Song By Grace We learn to Sing, and in Glory We Continue to Sing."

"I do not come into this pulpit hoping that perhaps somebody will of his own free will return to Christ. My hope lies in another quarter. I hope that my Master will lay hold of some of them and say, "You are mine, and you shall be mine. I claim you for myself. " My hope arises from the freeness of grace, and not from the freedom of the will."

"There, poor sinner, take my garment, and put it on; you shall stand before God as if you were Christ, and I will stand before God as if I had been the sinner; I will suffer in the sinner's stead, and you shall be rewarded for works that you did not do, but which I did for you."

"I would go to the deeps a hundred times to cheer a downcast spirit. It is good for me to have been afflicted, that I might know how to speak a word in season to one that is weary."

"You cannot slander human nature;
it is worse than words can paint it."

"If I were a Roman Catholic, I should turn a heretic, in sheer desperation, because I would rather go to heaven than go to purgatory."

"To rejoice in temporal comforts is dangerous, to rejoice in self is foolish, to rejoice in sin is fatal, but to rejoice in God is heavenly."

"No stars gleam as brightly as those which glisten in the polar sky. No water tastes so sweet as that which springs amid the desert sand. And no faith is so precious as that which lives and triumphs through adversity. Tested faith brings experience. You would never have believed your own weakness had you not needed to pass through trials. And you would never have known God's strength had His strength not been needed to carry you through."

"The Devil has seldom done a cleverer thing that hinting to the Church that part of their mission is to provide entertainment for the people, with a view to winning them. Providing amusement for the people is nowhere spoken of in the Scriptures as a function of the Church. The need is biblical doctrine, so understood and felt that is sets men afire."

"As for His failing you, never dream of it - hate the thought of it. The God who has been sufficient until now, should be trusted to the end."

"The goose that lays the golden eggs likes to lay where there are eggs already."

"We have come to a turning point in the road. If we turn to the right mayhap our children and our children's children will go that way; but if we turn to the left, generations yet unborn will curse our names for having been unfaithful to God and to His Word."

"Do not look to your hope, but to Jesus, the Source of your hope."

"Evil things are easy things: for they are natural to our fallen nature. Right things are rare flowers that need cultivation."

"There are no crown-wearers in heaven who were not cross-bearers here below."

"Jesus Christ does not save the worthy, but the unworthy. Your plea must not be righteousness but guilt."

"We might preach till our tongues rotted, till we should exhaust our lungs and die, but never a soul would be converted unless there were mysterious power going with it - the Holy Ghost changing the will of man. O Sirs! We might as well preach to stone walls as preach to humanity unless the Holy Ghost be with the word, to give it power to convert the soul."

"Death is the waiting-room where we robe ourselves for immortality."

"If any man is not sure that he is in Christ, he ought not to be easy one moment until he is sure. Dear friend, without the fullest confidence as to your saved condition, you have no right to be at ease, and I pray you may never be so. This is a matter too important to be left undecided."

"Hold everything earthly with a loose hand, but grasp eternal things with a death-like grip."

"Where God works, He works with men that work."

"If we had to preach to thousands year after year, and never rescued but one soul, that one soul would be a full reward for all our labour, for a soul is of countless price."

"Amusement should be used to do us good "like a medicine": it must never be used as the food of the man. Many have had all holy thoughts and gracious resolutions stamped out by perpetual trifling. Pleasure so called is the murderer of thought. This is the age of excessive amusement: everybody craves for it, like a babe for its rattle."

"Grace is the mother and nurse of holiness, and not the apologist of sin."

"Oh my brethren, Bold hearted men are always called mean-spirited by cowards!"

"The ungodly are not half so restrained in their blasphemy as we are in our praise."

"Wisdom is the right use of knowledge."

"Suffering is better than sinning. There is more evil in a drop of sin than in an ocean of affliction. Better, burn for Christ, than turn from Christ."

"The truest lengthening of life is to live while we live, wasting no time but using every hour for the highest ends. So be it this day."

"All originality and no plagiarism
makes for dull preaching."

"The tears of affliction are often needed to keep the eye of faith bright."

"Let each one of us, if we have done nothing for Christ, begin to do something now. The distribution of tracts is the first thing."

"The resurrection of Jesus Christ from the dead is one of the best attested facts on record. There were so many witnesses to behold it, that if we do in the least degree receive the credibility of men's testimonies, we cannot and we dare not doubt that Jesus rose from the dead."

"I do not believe that any man can preach the gospel who does not preach the Law. The Law is the needle, and you cannot draw the silken thread of the gospel through a man's heart unless you first send the needle of the Law to make way for it."

"If there be a man before me who says that the wrath of God is too heavy a punishment for his little sin, I ask him, if the sin be little, why does he not give it up?"

"You are not mature if you have a high esteem of yourself. He who boasts in himself is but a babe in Christ, if indeed he be in Christ at all. Young Christians may think much of themselves. Growing Christians think themselves nothing. Mature Christians know that they are less than nothing. The more holy we are, the more we mourn our infirmities, and the humbler is our estimate of ourselves."

"I would rather believe a limited atonement that is efficacious for all men for whom it was intended, than a universal atonement that is not efficacious for anybody, except the will of men be added to it."

"Humility is to make a right estimate of one's self."

"Men will never be great in theology until they are great in suffering."

"I have heard of some good old woman in a cottage, who had nothing but a piece of bread and a little water, and lifting up her hands, she said, as a blessing, What! all this, and Christ too?"

"Beloved, can you feel assured that
He carried your sin?"

"Saving faith is an immediate relation to Christ, accepting, receiving, resting upon Him alone, for justification, sanctification, and eternal life by virtue of God's grace."

"Faith is the silver thread upon which the pearls of the graces are to be hung. Break that, and you have broken the string - the pearls lie scattered on the ground."

"Fits of depression come over the most of us. Usually cheerful as we may be, we must at intervals be cast down. The strong are not always vigorous, the wise not always ready, the brave not always courageous, and the joyous not always happy."

"Christ will be master of the heart, and sin must be mortified. If your life is unholy, then your heart is unchanged, and you are an unsaved person. The Savior will sanctify His people, renew them, give them a hatred of sin, and a love of holiness. The grace that does not make a man better than others is a worthless counterfeit. Christ saves His people, not IN their sins, but FROM their sins. Without holiness, no man shall see the Lord."

"Prayer is an art which only the Spirit can teach us. He is the giver of all prayer."

"The worst forms of depression are cured when Holy Scripture is believed."

"The motto of all true servants of God must be, 'We preach Christ; and him crucified.' A sermon without Christ in it is like a loaf of bread without any flour in it. No Christ in your sermon, sir? Then go home, and never preach again until you have something worth preaching."

"Reckon then that to acquire soul-winning power, you will have to go through mental torment and soul distress. You must go into the fire if you are going to pull others out of it, and you will have to dive into the floods if you are going to draw others out of the water. You cannot work a fire escape without feeling the scorch of the conflagration, nor man a lifeboat without being covered with the waves."

"Carve your name on hearts, not on marble."

"If there is any verse that you would like left out of the Bible, that is the verse that ought to stick to you, like a blister, until you really attend to its teaching."

"If you meet with a system of theology which magnifies man, flee from it as far as you can."

"If you were God's children you would loathe the very thought of the world's evil joys, and your question would not be, "How far may we be like the world?" but your one cry would be, "How far can we get away from the world? How much can we come out from it?"

"I long for nothing more earnestly than to serve God with all my might."

"Death is no punishment to the believer: it is the gate of endless joy."

"We are too prone to engrave our trials in marble and write our blessings in sand."

"A church should be a camp of soldiers, not an hospital of invalids. But there is exceedingly much difference between what ought be and what is, and consequently many of God's people are in so sad a state that the very fittest prayer for them is for revival."

"Let your thoughts be psalms, your prayers incense, and your breath praise."

"He that buildeth his nest upon a Divine promise shall find it abide and remain until he shall fly away to the land where promises are lost in fulfillments."

"Unbelief will destroy the best of us;
faith will save the worst of us."

"It is only serving God that is doing immortal work; it is only living for Christ that is living at all."

"Obedience to the will of God is the pathway to perpetual honor and everlasting joy."

"In seasons of severe trial, the Christian has nothing on earth that he can trust to, and is therefore compelled to cast himself on God alone. When no human deliverance can avail, he must simply and entirely trust himself to the providence and care of God. Happy storm that wrecks a man on such a rock as this! O blessed hurricane that drives the soul to God-and God alone!"

"If you love anything better than God you are idolaters: if there is anything you would not give up for God it is your idol: if there is anything that you seek with greater fervor than you seek the glory of God, that is your idol, and conversion means a turning from every idol."

"Abide close to the cross, and search the mystery of His wounds."

"Habits, soft and pliant at first, are like some coral stones, which are easily cut when first quarried, but soon become hard as adamant."

"No matter how good you think yourself to be, you cannot enter heaven unless it is under the terms of sovereign grace."

"The Spirit of God bears no witness to Christless sermons. Leave Jesus out of your preaching, and the Holy Spirit will never come upon you. Why should he? Has he not come on purpose that he may testify of Christ? Did not Jesus say, 'He shall glorify me: for he shall receive of mine, and shall show it unto you'? Yes, the subject was Christ, and nothing but Christ, and such is the teaching which the Spirit of God will own. Be it ours never to wander from this central point: may we determine to know nothing among men but Christ and his cross."

"The marvel of heaven and earth, of time and eternity, is the atoning death of Jesus Christ. This is the mystery that brings more glory to God than all creation."

"That crafty kindness which inveigles me to sacrifice principle is the serpent in the grass - deadly to the incautious wayfarer."

"Praise is the rehearsal for our eternal song."

"The greatest joy of a Christian is to give joy to Christ."

"Be not proud of race, face, place, or grace."

"He who does not hate the false does not love the true; and he to whom it is all the same whether it be God's word or man's, is himself unrenewed at heart."

"Faith is reason at rest in God."

"When we believe that God hears us, it is but natural that we should be eager to hear Him. Only from Him can come the word which can speak peace to troubled spirits; the voices of men are feeble in such a case, a plaster far too narrow for the sore; but God's voice is power, He speaks and it is done, and hence when we hear Him our distress is ended."

"A high character might be produced, I suppose, by continued prosperity, but it has very seldom been the case. Adversity, however it may appear to be our foe, is our true friend; and, after a little acquaintance with it, we receive it as a precious thing - the prophecy of a coming joy. It should be no ambition of ours to traverse a path without a thorn or stone."

"Serve God with integrity, and if you achieve no success, at least no sin will lie upon your conscience."

"You have no time for the prayer meeting, but you have time enough to be brushing your hair to all eternity; you have no time to bend your knee, but plenty of time to make yourselves look smart and grand."

"May we live here like strangers and make the world not a house, but an inn, in which we sup and lodge, expecting to be on our journey tomorrow."

"Prayer must not be our chance work but our daily business, our habit and vocation."

"We ought not to tolerate for a minute the ghastly and grievous thought that God will not answer prayer."

"The Providence of God is the great protector of our life and usefulness, and under the divine care we are perfectly safe from danger."

"Nothing teaches us about the preciousness of the Creator as much as when we learn the emptiness of everything else."

"Your emptiness is but the preparation for your being filled, and your casting down is but the making ready for your lifting up."

"Serve God by doing common actions in a heavenly spirit, and then, if your daily calling only leaves you cracks and crevices of time, fill them up with holy service."

"Immanuel, God with us in our nature, in our sorrow, in our lifework, in our punishment, in our grave, and now with us, or rather we with Him, in resurrection, ascension, triumph, and Second Advent splendor."

"Gospel riches are sent to remove our wretchedness, and mercy to remove our misery."

"If you think you can walk in holiness without keeping up perpetual fellowship with Christ, you have made a great mistake. If you would be holy, you must live close to Jesus."

"You must be in fashion is the utterance of weak headed mortals."

"If we empty our hearts of self God will fill them with His love."

"When I have found intense pain relieved, a weary brain soothed, and calm refreshing sleep obtained by a cigar, I have felt grateful to God, and have blessed His name."

"Soul-serving requires a heart that beats hard against the ribs. It requires a soul full of the milk of human kindness. This is the sine qua non of success."

"Delayed answers to prayer are not only trials of faith; they also give us opportunities to honor God through our steadfast confidence in Him, even when facing the apparent denial of our request."

"Show me 12 drunkards and I will show you 12 nagging wives."

"Our motto is, "With God, anywhere: without God, nowhere. "."

"The child of God works not for life, but from life; he does not work to be saved, but works because he is saved."

"A child of five, if properly instructed, can, as truly believe, and be regenerated, as an adult."

"To know is not to be wise. To know how to use knowledge is to have wisdom."

"It is better to preach five words of God's Word than five million words of man's wisdom."

"Too many people write their blessings in the sand but engrave their sorrows in marble."

"Live and die without prayer, and you will pray long enough when you get to hell."

"Since, O sweet Lord Jesus, Thou art the present portion of Thy people, favour us this year with such a sense of Thy preciousness, that from its first to its last day we may be glad and rejoice in Thee. Let January open with joy in the Lord, and December close with gladness in Jesus."

"Our best performances are so stained with sin, that it is hard to know whether they are good works or bad works."

"If I had only one more sermon to preach before I died, it would be about my Lord Jesus Christ. And I think that when we get to the end of our ministry, one of our regrets will be that we did not preach more of him."

"The friend of God must not spend a day without God, and he must undertake no work apart from his God."

"Obedience is the highest practical courage."

"Sanctification grows out of faith in Jesus Christ. Reemember holiness is a flower, not a root; it is not sanctification that saves, but salvation that sanctifies."

"I have my own opinion that there is no such thing as preaching Christ and Him crucified, unless we preach what nowadays is called Calvinism. It is a nickname to call it Calvinism; Calvinism is the gospel, and nothing else."

"There is dust enough on some of your Bibles to write 'damnation' with your fingers."

"Show the world that your God is worth ten thousand worlds to you. Show rich men how rich you are in your poverty when the Lord God is your helper. Show the strong man how strong you are in your weakness when underneath you are the everlasting arms."

"Self-righteousness exclaims, "I will not be saved in God's way; I will make a new road to heaven; I will not bow before God's grace; I will not accept the atonement which God has wrought out in the person of Jesus; I will be my own redeemer; I will enter heaven by my own strength, and glorify my own merits. " The Lord is very wroth against self-righteousness. I do not know of anything against which His fury burneth more than against this, because this touches Him in a very tender point, it insults the glory and honor of His Son Jesus Christ."

"Satan does not care whether he drags you down to hell as a Calvinist or as an Arminian, so long as he can get you there."

"A Christian man should so shine in his life, that a person could not live with him a week without knowing the gospel."

"So long as we are receivers of mercy, we must be givers of thanks."

"If it does not glorify Christ, let it not console or please you."

"God will not be absent when His people are on trial; he will stand in court as their advocate, to plead on their behalf."

"This is now a covenant of pure grace; let no man attempt to mix works with it."

"In all of my years of service to my Lord, I have discovered a truth that has never failed and has never been compromised. That truth is that it is beyond the realm of possibilities that one has the ability to out-give God. Even if I give the whole of my worth to Him, He will find a way to give back to me much more than I gave."

"Many books in my library are now behind and beneath me. They were good in their way once, and so were the clothes I wore when I was ten years old; but I have outgrown them. Nobody ever outgrows Scripture; the book widens and deepens with our years."

"Beloved, there are heights in experimental knowledge of the things of God that the eagles discerning eye and philosophical thought have never seen. God alone can take us there, but the chariot in which He takes us up and the fiery steeds that pull the chariot, are prevailing prayers."

"A man who knows that he is saved by believing in Christ does not, when he is baptized, lift his baptism into a saving ordinance. In fact, he is the very best protester against that mistake, because he holds that he has no right to be baptized until he is saved."

"The greatest and most momentous
fact which
the history of the world records is
the fact of-Christ's birth."

"Character is always lost when a high ideal is sacrificed on the altar of conformity and popularity."

"If God has fit you to be a missionary, I would not have you shrivel down to be a king."

"If you are renewed by grace, and were to meet your old self, I am sure you would be very anxious to get out of his company."

"Sorrow for sin should be the keenest sorrow; joy in the Lord should be the loftiest joy."

"Our joy ends where love of the world begins."

"Blessed are the peacemakers, and one sure way of peacemaking is to let the fire of contention alone. Neither fan it, nor stir it, nor add fuel to it, but let it go out by itself. Begin your ministry with one blind eye and one deaf ear."

"I would rather lay my soul asoak in half a dozen verses [of the Bible] all day than rinse my hand in several chapters."

"God gave me this great book to preach from, and if He has put anything in it you think is not fit, go and complain to Him, not to me. I am simply his servant, and if His errand that I am to tell is objectionable, I cannot help it."

"In 40 years I have not spent 15 minutes without thinking of Jesus."

"Never be afraid of the world's censure; it's praise is much more to be dreaded."

"Whether we like it or not, asking is the rule of the kingdom."

"A true prayer is an inventory of needs, a catalog of necessities, an exposure of secret wounds, a revelation of hidden poverty."

"Is there nothing to sing about to-day? Then borrow a song from tomorrow; sing of what is yet to be. Is this world dreary? Then think of the next."

"Conversion is a turning onto the right road. The next thing to do is to walk on it."

"Humility makes us ready to be blessed by the God of all grace."

"He who will not use the thoughts of other men's brains proves that he has no brains of his own."

"Oh, the stoop of the Redeemer's amazing love! Let us, henceforth, contend how low we can go side by side with Him, but remember when we have gone to the lowest He descends lower still, so that we can truly feel that the very lowest place is too high for us, because He has gone lower still."

"As the salt flavors every drop in the Atlantic, so does sin affect every atom of our nature. It is so sadly there, so abundantly there, that if you cannot detect it, you are deceived."

"Watch constantly against those things which are thought to be no temptations. The most poisonous serpents are found where the sweetest flowers grow. Cleopatra was poisoned by an asp that was brought to her in a basket of fair flowers. Sharp-edged tools, long handled, wound at last."

"There is no fatigue so wearisome as that which comes from lack of work."

"Methinks every true Christian should be exceedingly earnest in prayer concerning the souls of the ungodly; and when they are so, how abundantly God blesses them and how the church prospers!"

"A good character is the best
tombstone."

"There should be a parallel between our supplications and our thanksgivings. We ought not to leap in prayer, and limp in praise."

"We must trust as if it all depended on God and work as if it all depended on us."

"Holy service in constant fellowship
with God is heaven below."

"He who fears God has nothing else to fear."

"Whatever is your greatest joy and treasure, that is your god."

"There are, in truth, but two denominations upon this earth: the Church and the world."

"Grace puts its hand on the boasting mouth, and shuts it once for all."

"Intercessory prayer is an act of communion with Christ, for Jesus pleads for the sons of men."

"Men are in a restless pursuit after satisfaction and earthly things. They have no forethought for their eternal state, the present hour absorbs them. They turn to another and another of earth's broken cisterns, hoping to find water, where not a drop was ever discovered yet."

"Every time you prefer the pleasures of this world to the joys of heaven, you spit in the face of Christ; every time when to gain in your business, you do an unrighteous thing, you are like Judas selling Him for thirty pieces of silver; every time you make a false profession of religion, you give Him a traitor's kiss; every word you have spoken against Him, every hard thought you have had of Him, has helped to complete your complicity with the great crowd which gathered around the Cross of Calvary, to mock and jeer the Lord of life and glory."

"Little learning and much pride
come of hasty reading."

"Whenever GOD determines to do a great work, HE first sets HIS people to pray."

"Do not become self-sufficient . Self-sufficienc y is Satan's net where he catches men, like poor silly fish, and destroys them. Be not self-sufficient . The way to grow strong in Christ is to become weak in yourself. God pours no power into man's heart till man's power is all poured out. Live, then, daily, a life of dependence on the grace of God."

"Ah! dear friend,
you little know the possibilities
which are in you."

"The right way usually lies between two extremes: it is the narrow channel between the rock and the whirlpool."

"The fact is, brethren, we must have conversion work here. We cannot go on as some churches do without converts. We cannot, we will not, we must not, we dare not. Souls must be converted here, and if there be not many born to Christ, may the Lord grant to me that I may sleep in the tomb and be heard no more. Better indeed for us to die than to live, if souls be not saved."

"Long ago I ceased to count heads. Truth is usually in the minority in this evil world."

"You will never know God's strength until He has supported you in deep waters."

"No life can surpass that of a man who quietly continues to serve God in the place where providence has placed him."

"We often forget that the author of our faith must be the finisher of it also."

"If we give God service it must be because He gives us grace. We work for Him because He works in us."

"Let us measure ourselves by our Master, and not by our fellow-servants : then pride will be impossible."

"You cannot have Christ, if you will not serve Him."

"Quietude, which some men cannot abide because it reveals their inward poverty, is as a palace of cedar to the wise, for along its hallowed courts the King in his beauty deigns to walk."

"Let me revel in this one thought: before God made the heavens and the earth, He set His love upon me."

"Secularism teaches us that we ought to look to this world. Christianity teaches us that the best way to prepare for this world is to be fully prepared for the next."

"True prayer is the trading of the heart with God, and the heart never comes into spiritual commerce with the ports of heaven until God the Holy Ghost puts wind into the sails and speeds the ship into its haven."

"To me, Calvinism means the placing of the eternal God at the head of all things."